Reese's pieces

Peanut Butter

CANDY IN A CRUNCHY SHELL

Count by Tens

by Jerry Pallotta
Illustrated by Rob Bolster

SCHOLASTIC INC.

New York   Toronto   London   Auckland   Sydney   Mexico City   New Delhi   Hong Kong   Buenos Aires

Thank you to Annie, Betty, Fuzzy, and Zack!
—— *Jerry Pallotta*

This book is dedicated to all artists who honor their gift by never quitting.
—— *Rob Bolster*

OFFICIAL
HERSHEY'S®
LICENSED PRODUCT

ISBN 0-439-63990-5

12 11 10 9 8 7 6 5 4 3 2 1   4 5 6 7 8 9/0

Printed in the U.S.A.
First printing, September 2004

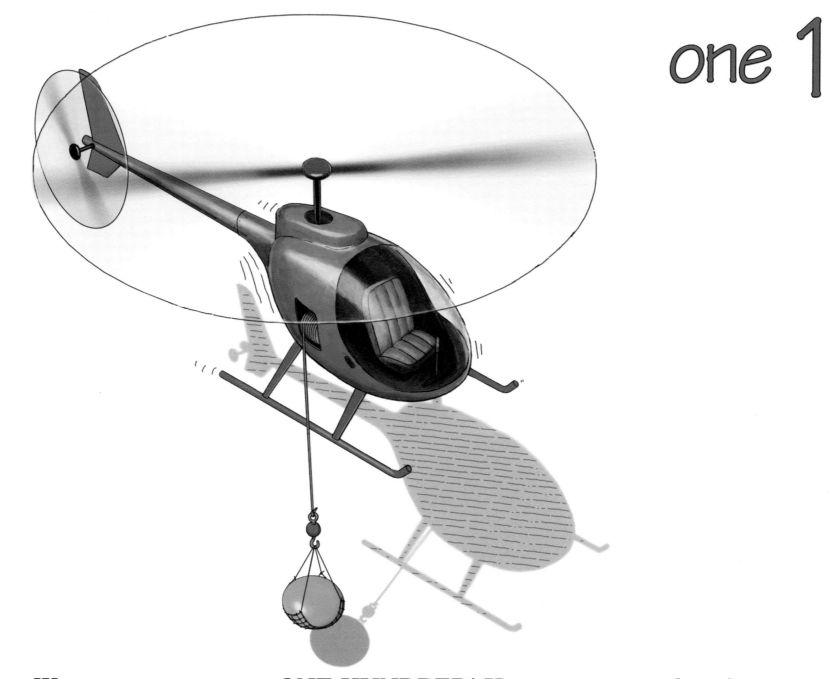

We are on our way to ONE HUNDRED! How can we get there?
We are going to count by TENS. First, let's count from one to ten,
one candy at a time. We are now at the number ONE.
The helicopter will take us to the next number.

2 two

Here we are at the number TWO.
The boat will take us across the water to the next number.
As you count, think of different ways to travel.

The next number on our way to ten is THREE.
An orange, a yellow, and a brown REESE'S PIECES® are being loaded on the jet.
Hop aboard—we will fly to the next number!

4 four

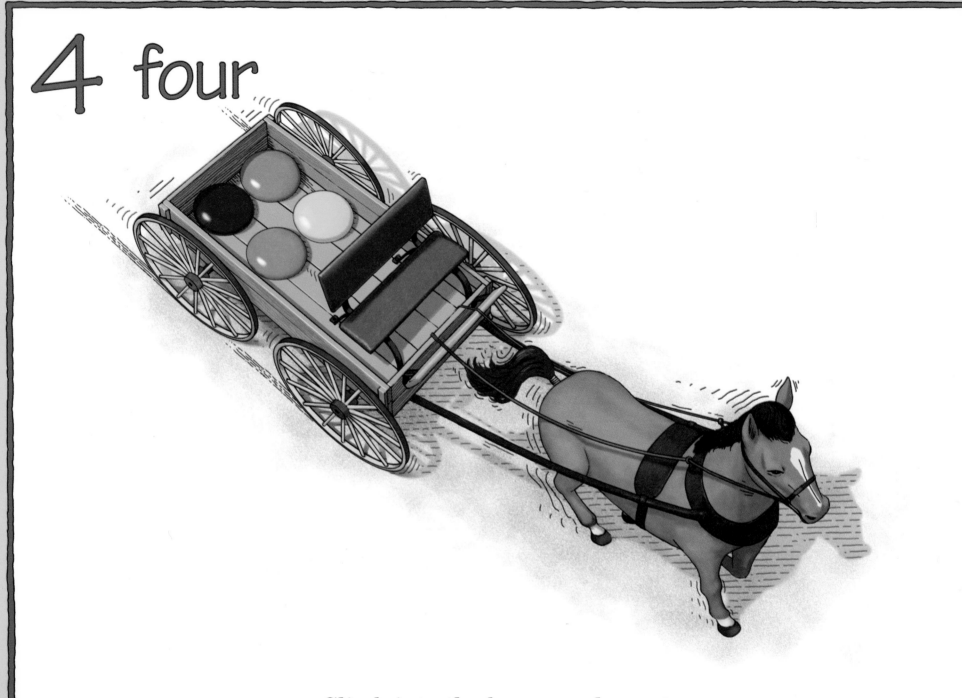

Climb into the buggy and count.
One, two, three, FOUR candies. There are four wheels on the buggy.
How many legs does a horse have?

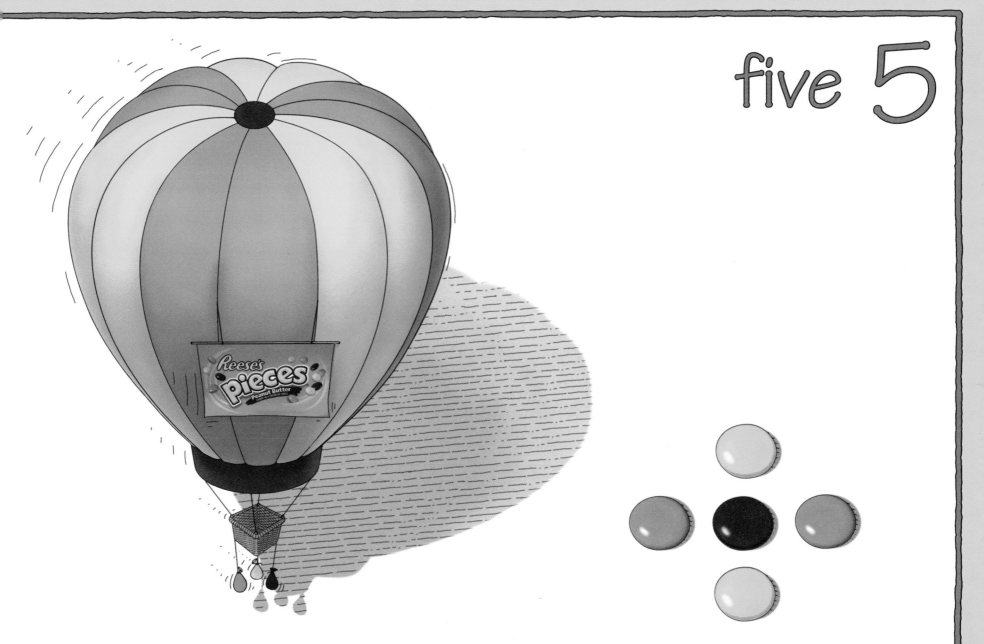

The horse pulled us to the number FIVE.
Now you'll go up, up, and away in this hot air balloon.
Float over to the next number.

6 six

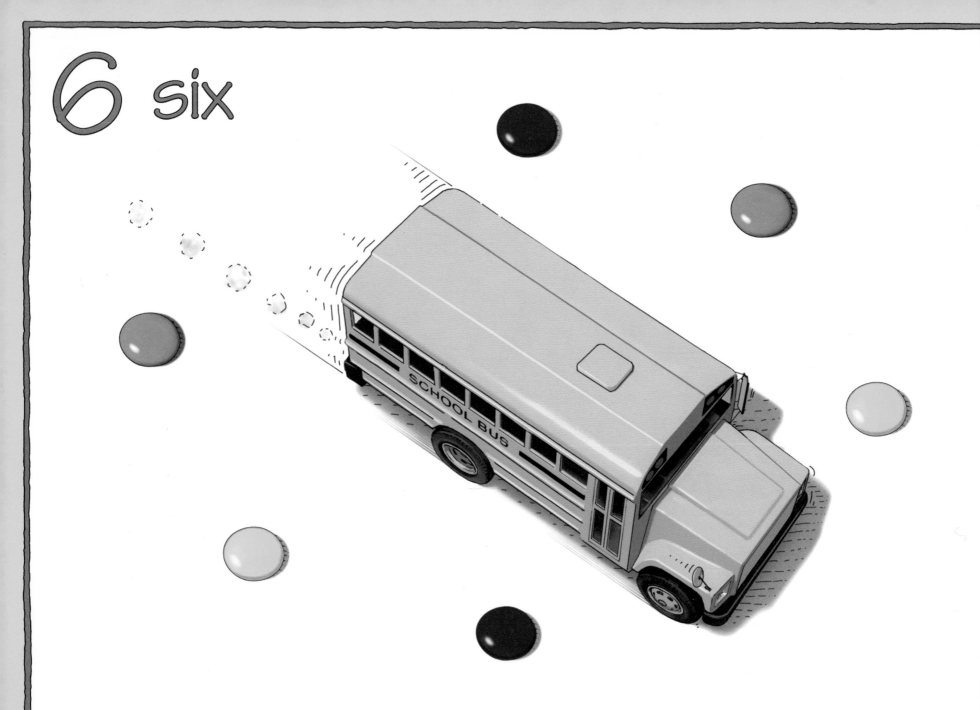

Beep! Beep! It is time for school.
Don't miss the bus! Add one more piece of candy and count.
One, two, three, four, five, SIX!

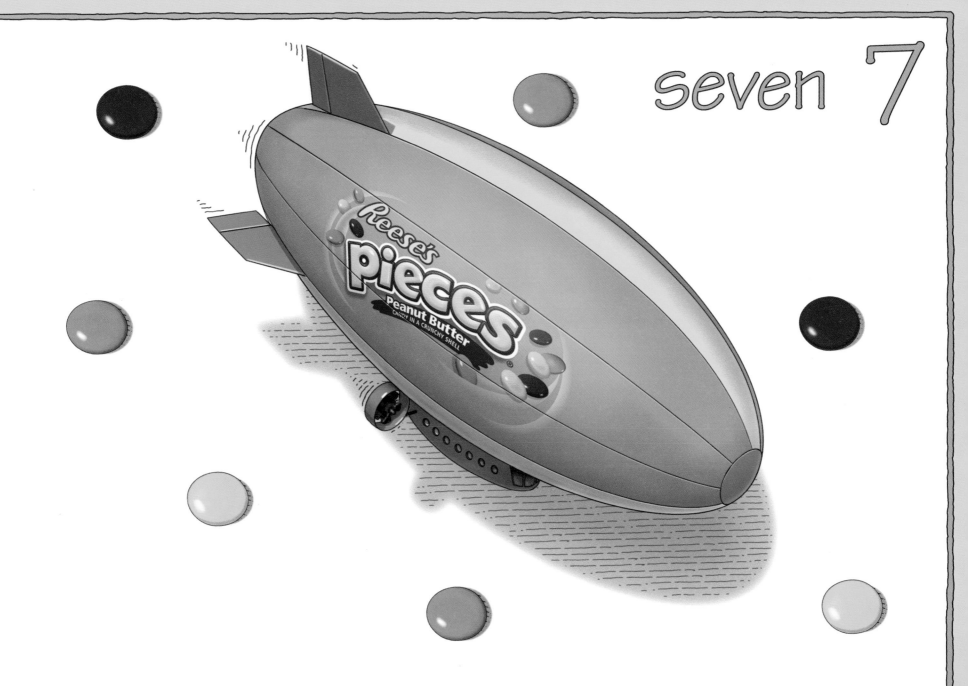

This is your chance to fly in a blimp.
Count the SEVEN candies.
Then grab the controls and fly to the next number.

8 eight

All aboard! All aboard! Get your tickets!
The train is leaving the station.
One, two, three, four, five, six, seven, EIGHT!

Now we are at the number NINE!
Start pedaling the bicycle. Don't stop until you get to the number ten.

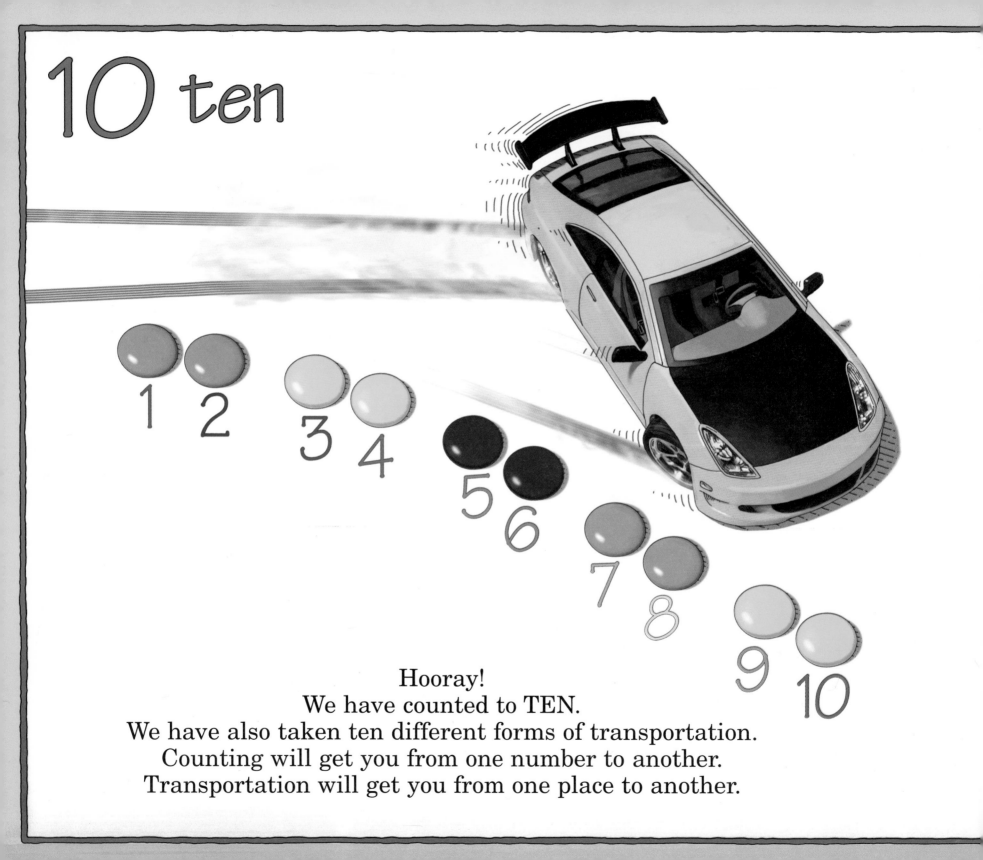

10 ten

1 2 3 4 5 6 7 8 9 10

Hooray!
We have counted to TEN.
We have also taken ten different forms of transportation.
Counting will get you from one number to another.
Transportation will get you from one place to another.

ten 10

10

9

8

7

6

5

4

3

2

1

Put the sports car in reverse!
Do a review.
Just use one color. Count again!
One, two, three, four, five, six, seven, eight, nine, TEN!
We made one group of ten.

20 twenty

Now we are going to count to one hundred by tens.

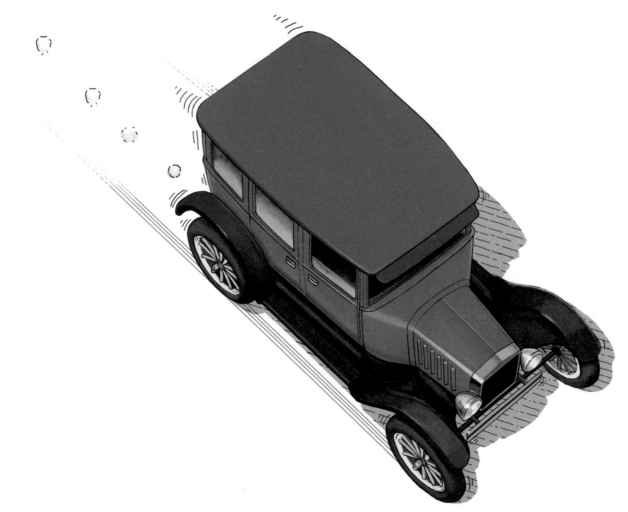

When counting by tens, the next number is not eleven.
This old Model T takes us to TWENTY!

Put the candy in groups of ten.

Count each group.

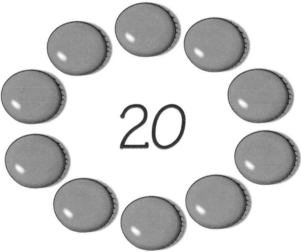

Ten, TWENTY! Grouping makes counting easier.

30 thirty

A golf cart is another way to get around.

Wait — this is no time for sports!
We are learning to count by tens.

Here is one orange group, one brown group, and one yellow group.

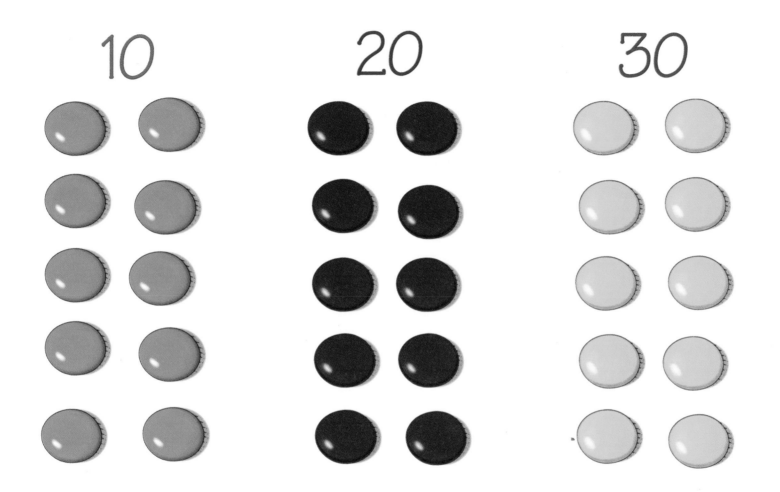

Grouping by colors makes sense.
It is simple! One, two, three. Ten, twenty, THIRTY!

40 forty

Zoom in low and count to FORTY.

Flying in a biplane is faster than walking.
Counting by tens is faster than counting by ones.

Ten, twenty, thirty, FORTY!

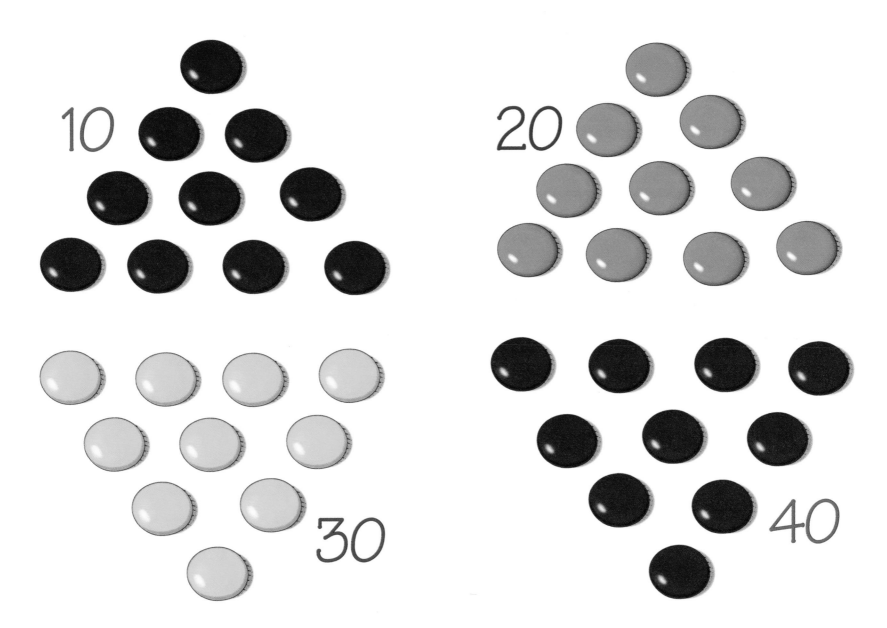

Can you think of other ways to get from one place to another?

50 fifty

Let's celebrate and take a cruise.

FIFTY! We are halfway to one hundred.
It's as easy as one, two, three, four, five.

Ten, twenty, thirty, forty, FIFTY!

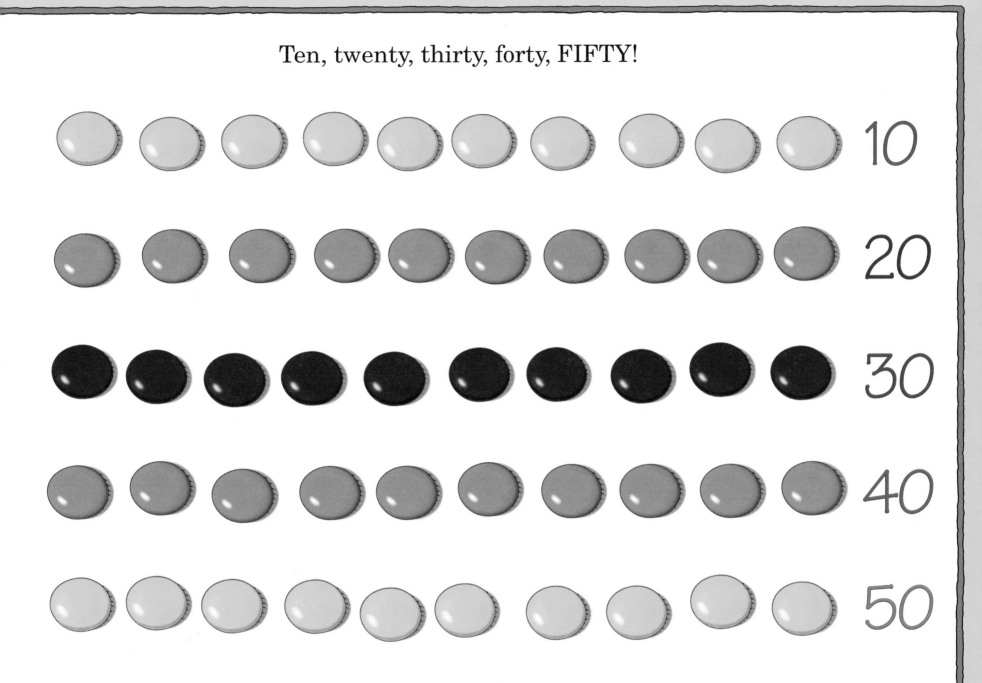

We already made groups shaped like circles, rectangles, and triangles.
Here are groups in a straight line. The shape of each group does not matter.
The number of pieces in each group is what is important.

60 sixty

Taxi! Taxi!
Take us to the next number.

Hop in back. Relax! Let someone else do the driving.
But please keep on counting.

Each of these six groups is multicolored.

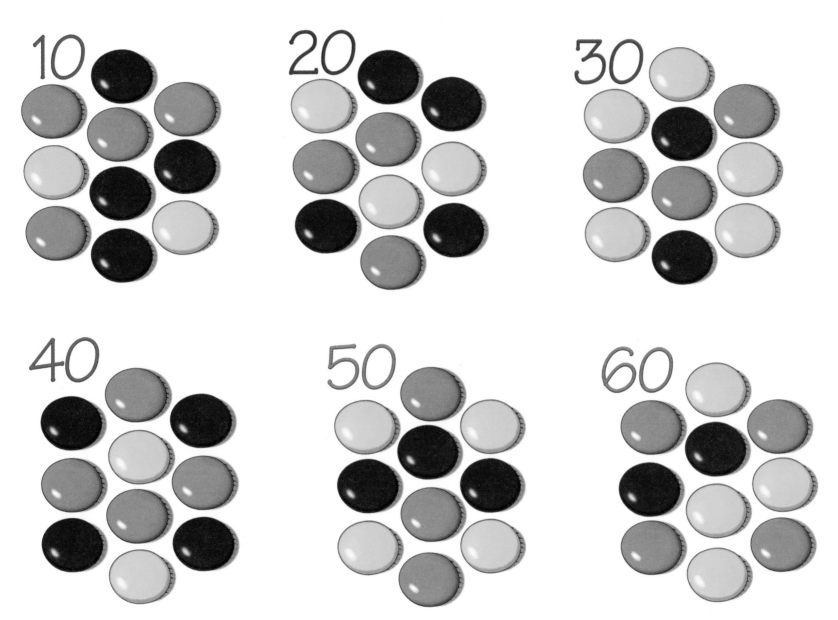

We are counting candy. Color does not matter.
Remember, the number of pieces in each group is what is important.
Ten, twenty, thirty, forty, fifty, SIXTY!

70 seventy

And now for some monster tires!

A pickup truck is another way to travel.
Motor yourself to the number SEVENTY.

Never give up! Keep on going, keep on counting.

Ten, twenty, thirty, forty, fifty, sixty, SEVENTY! Here are seven groups.
You could say there are seven sets, or seven bunches.

80 eighty

Put on your space suit!
Take the space shuttle to EIGHTY!

We are on a mission — counting by tens to one hundred!

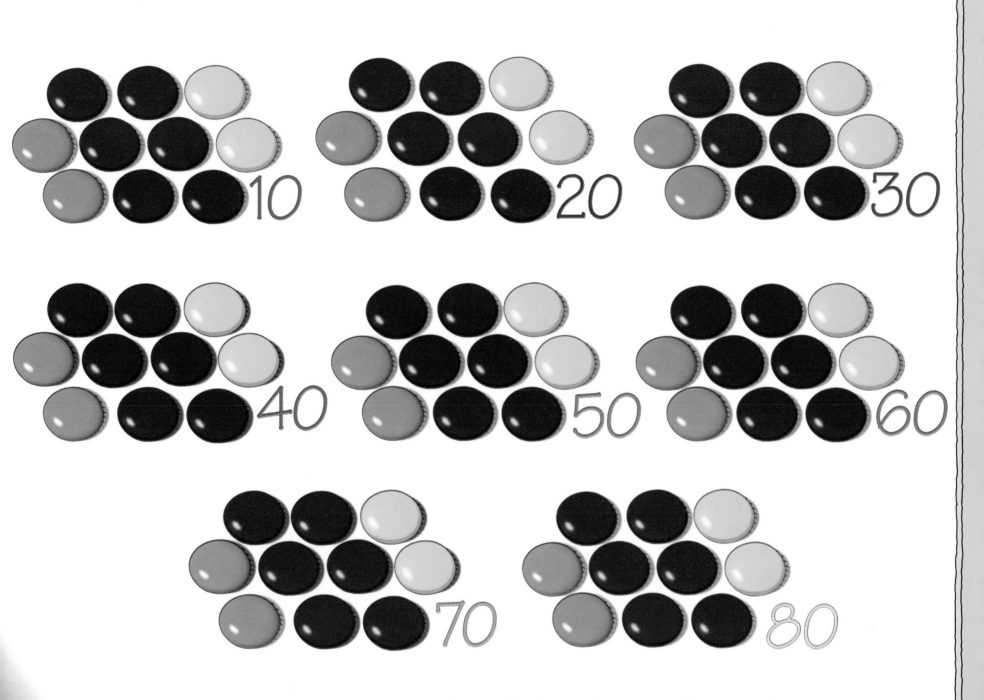

When you count by tens, you skip all the other numbers in between. Think of other ways to count. We could make groups of two, groups of three, groups of four, or groups of five.

90 ninety

In freezing, snowy weather,
a dogsled team is the best way to go.

Mush your way to NINETY!

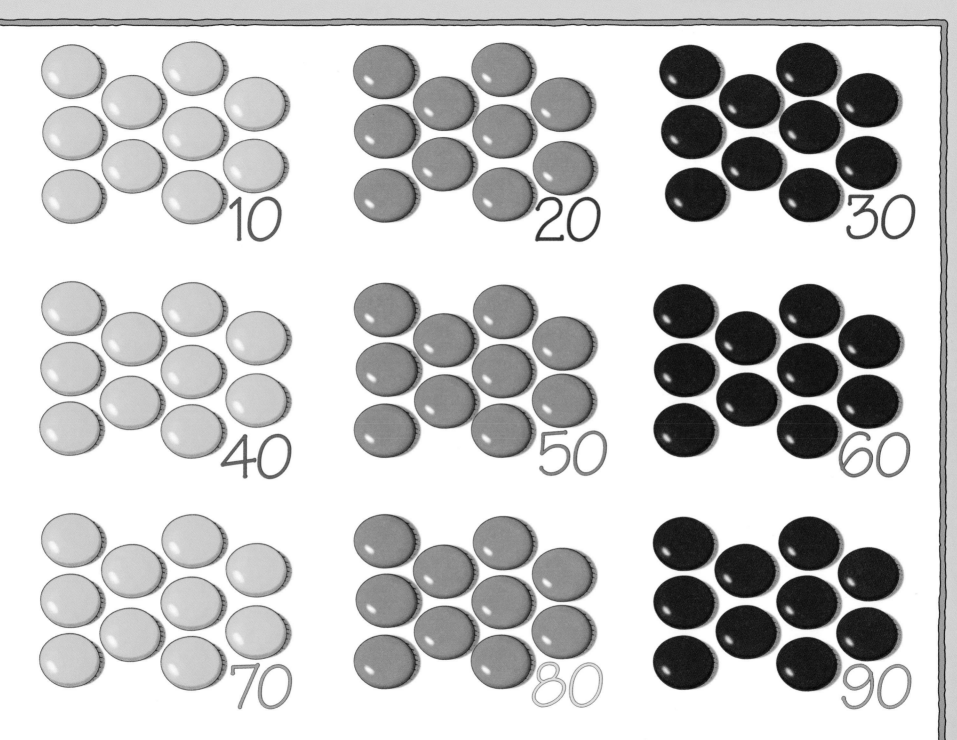

Count out ten more candies for another group.
One, two, three, four, five, six, seven, eight, nine, ten. Now we are at NINETY!
Only ten more candies in a group, and we will get to one hundred.

100 one hundred

We made it to ONE HUNDRED!

Counting by tens helped us reach one hundred really quickly.
It was as if we were speeding in a dragster.

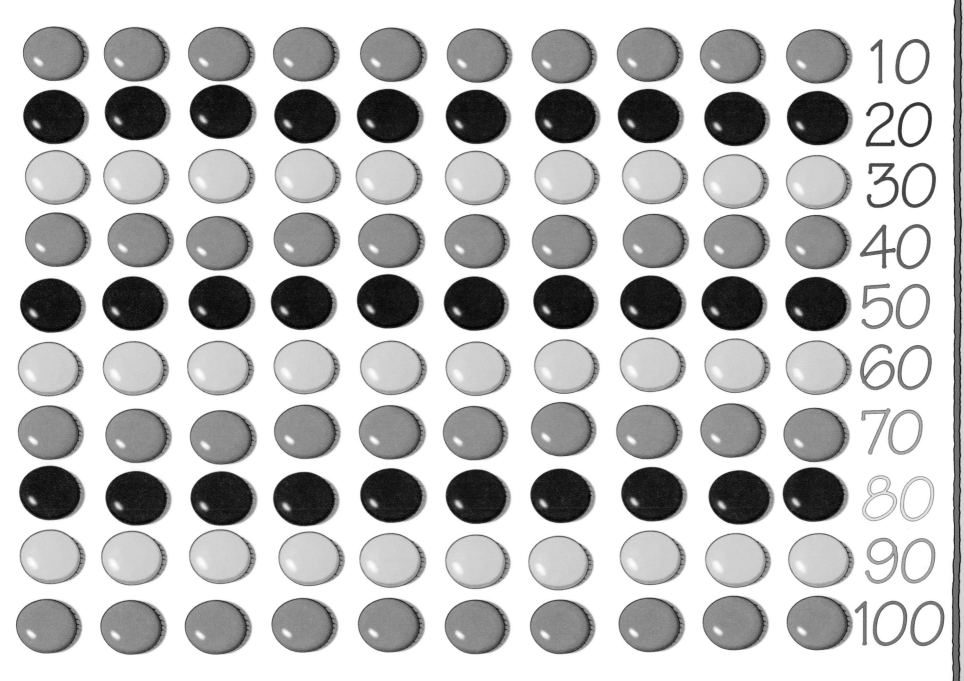

10
20
30
40
50
60
70
80
90
100

Rev up your engines. While the tires are screeching, practice!
Ten, twenty, thirty, forty, fifty, sixty, seventy, eighty, ninety, ONE HUNDRED!
Grouping and counting by tens makes math fun!

100
90
80 70 60
50
40
30 20 10 0

Hop on this unicycle and count by tens again.
This time do it backward.

One hundred, ninety, eighty, seventy, sixty, fifty, forty, thirty, twenty, ten, ZERO!
There are zero pieces of candy on this page!